The Strife And Rhymes Of A Lifetime (vol.3)

Richard Greenlow

ISBN: 9798516803895

DEDICATION

To my one and only Betsy; my muse, my strife & rhymes, my everything…

This book is for you, my twin-flame soulmate.

I've always known you, and it is an honour and privilege to be a part of your life.

Long live the Queen!

"Among the great geniuses of our time, all showed a readiness to discard prevalent views, an irreverence toward established authority, and a 'psychological unease', which could cause mental trouble such as depression, anxiety or alcoholism. But if these qualities were not too incapacitating, they actually contributed to the individuals ability to achieve significant creativity, blaze new trails, propose radical solutions and promote new schools of thought"

Arnold Ludwig, from his book entitled "The Price Of Greatness".

CONTENTS

ACKNOWLEDGMENTS

To my children, Nathaniel George, Chantelle-Marie, Allyssa-Leigh: endless love goes out to you all. Live your lives as if there will be no tomorrow, I save all my wishes for you. To Steve and George: you guys have been a blessing. Getting to know you has filled me with hope and I look forward to seeing more of you in the future. To my dear, late Gran: thank you for blessing me with this gift and encouraging me to get into print. To my nieces, nephew and granddaughter, how I miss seeing you. I am filled with hope that we will see much more of each other in the future. To my cousin Steve and family: blessings and love. To my cousin Marlon: can't wait to catch up with you. To everyone else: thank you for listening, supporting me and being a part of my strife and rhymes. Blessed Be.

1 MISSION STATEMENT : ADDENDUM

Unthreatened by the walls of Babylon
I stand my ground and stroll onwards to move on,
Weathering the storms atop the mountains,
Basking in the surety that we're definitely never parting.
Heavens above, I mean who would have thought it?
Masking the jagged edges and hidden wounds
Of the times we tried but had to climb out the other side,
In order to ride the incoming tide of silt.

Survival meant no relenting from the task ahead,
Vast energy spent trying hard to be better than the last,
When all it ever really needed was time and chance
To make our meeting come at the just the right moment.
Is the Universe gifting us immediate full-time employment?
We know it won't be easy and we know that it's gonna' hurt,
But these growing pains won't prevent the impending avalanche
Of spontaneous emotional growth that shines out from within.

The devil is indeed, once again, in the details
We know exactly what this life together entails,
Holding hands, holding up our side of the deal,
So that our chances of success become realer than real.
Never shirking or opting out of any row or disagreement,
For these are opportunities for us to challenge each other
Forget the idea of existing by yourself in a bubble,
When two become one in this way the whole world's in trouble,

Rest your weary head a while, have a little powernap,
You've more than earnt the time to gently lay your head.
Don't be misled though, sleep too long and it really hurts,
Knowing we may have lost time in the ongoing strive to rise.
Speak to me more, tell me of how I astound and amaze you,
And how proud you've become of the man I've spent so long becoming,
Carrying on in the same vein seems the most sane thing to do,
With all we're faced with from the past that still burns and stews.

Try not to fret when you regret things you may have fucked up,
Leave them in the past and re-learn lessons you learned from the start,
It's not our imperative to just get good, then stop and get lazy,
Some remembered days from back then are real wavy and hazy..
Behave just how you know your integrity throws out obvious signs of,
In order to walk the walk, walk outside and allow the world to see
The shining example of a man who really cares, strong in his skin,
No longer has a need to wonder off and be alone again.

Gratitude for all I construe as beautiful in this life that I'm living.
I'll keep on keeping on, keeping up the right song and dance..
The soundtrack to this life is one of variety abounding,
At times upbeat and at other times really dark-sounding.
Whatever weather currently threatens to rain on our parade,
We're automatically sheltered from all the worst effects,
Because of this endless and undying world of love that we share
Constantly learning lessons and resurrecting ourselves from despair.

R. C. Greenlow
[16.05.2020]

2 FAILED TO SEA

Shoelaces just came undone again,
Braces too loose to be of any use
Face is stooped towards the setting sun,
Case is closed, exposed to everyone.

Trouble is inevitably heading home,
Bubbling up behind, and in pursuit,
Muddled up memories on the smartphone
Reveal a figure dressed in a man-suit,
Flecks of orange puke stain his collar,
Every word heard from him is hollow
As he swallows what's left of his pride,
Keeping the poison deep down inside.

Hard to imagine anyone choosing
This kind of excuse for a life,
Yet choose it he did, he hid only behind
The same kind of disguise as us all
But his walls had to be dismantled
When he outgrew all that he knew,
Leaving him without boundaries
To contain his rising personality.

The reality suddenly hits home,
He's totally alone, broken phone,
Droning on about how he sinned
Everyone knows, blows with the wind.

Opinions matter not, hot blast
From past drafts of his script,
Ripped open, he's only joking
But toking spliffs like fury,
Waiting for the jury to retire,
Perspiring with that heat,
Plates of meat aching madly,
Sadly that's all he can seem
To do with his man-suit.

The judge appears, he hears
The verdict, silently, screams
And suddenly the show's over,
Never knew who he was
Because he failed to see
The calm patch of sea.

R C Greenlow
[27.01.2021]

3 FRENEMIES

Where did you go,
Slowly forming old illusion of me!
Old memory of what I used to be
Tell us all how deluded I was
To think I was really free.

I should have quit so much sooner,
But it soothes me to know I did it!
I kicked the shit before it killed me,
I'll tell the world how it thrills me
To be free of it all, truly.

So, friends, build no walls,
Hang murals of happy memories
Everywhere there's any space
We need to fill,
We still stand together, frenemies.

R C Greenlow
[04.02.2007]

4 RETROSPECTIVE REWIND

There's times I'm dreaming of,
Old-school days all blown away,
Replaced by new-age retrospect,
Enlarged by the hands of decay.

Fears upon fears had built up
And the icy grip of panic took ahold
We had become hopelessly lost,
Talking crap about feeling so old.

Layers of hatred plastered us,
Like thieves trapped by vigilantes
We were handcuffed to the weight of our hate
And told to be quiet and wait…

Now I'm looking ahead with conquered regret
Some people I love, others I simply just met,
Their images blend into a fanfare of dross
Now I've decided finally that I'm my own boss.

Life is a spiral of intrigue, enslaved by fear,
Constantly striving to find a way out of here.
Turn now the key to the lock, open your mind,
Let trust be your shield, the retrospective rewind.

R C Greenlow
[2001]

5 REFLECTIVE

Save me baby,
The gravy train I'm drowning in
Is in my brain, and now begins
The gurgling sound.
Please don't hear me drown,
I don't want you around.

Can't be alone tonight,
So frightening, knowing no one
Wants to see me fight myself,
Having to keep safe those I love
By not having them close
Is what truly hurts the most.

Done with anger, blame, remorse,
Regret, reflection and therapy.
What use is a solution
When what's needed is a remedy?
Don't try to tell me I need help,
I've always done this all by myself.

R C Greenlow
[06.07.2019]

6 EVER MINDFUL

When the wind cries not,
And the air pressure relents,
You vent the pent up negativity
Like a coiled spring finally released.
Tension can deafen the mind,
Dampen your hearts desire
And smother the fires of your soul
If left to get out of control.

Never let people invalidate you,
If your cause is good and true
You have every right to pursue
All avenues to get where you're going to.
As long as your ever mindful
Of other people's desire and needs
You can add beauty to life's garden
Trampling only on rubbish and weeds.

R C Greenlow
[28.03.2019]

7 TIME IS NOW

So it is! Struck by light;
Absolutely wonderful reflections
Surround the midnight hour
And bless us with insight,
So now we have to march,
The night is still young,
Things still need to be done.

This is our moment, now!
Forget the past, it's gone,
Listen now to our song
Echoing round the trees.

R C Greenlow
[05.06.2001]

8 MY OWN SICKNESS HURTS

I'm quite sure I'm finally at the start.
I don't have the answers, they elude me,
They chase me only round in circles in my mind,
Leaving me dizzy and nauseous and confused.
Looking out my window I only see mist,
Of days lost to summer and avoided dreams,
Winter catching up with a failure to succeed
In that which I've chosen as my goal.

Harder though it is to be hurting like this,
I'm glad that ignorance plays no part
In my life-script, my challenge is myself,
Alone with only my sickness to comfort me.
There is no room for anyone else in here,
I have enough trouble keeping myself contained,
No one asks me if I'm happy any more
Which is the way it has to be.

R C Greenlow
[30.07.2000]

9 OF TIMES GONE BY

Do you remember a time like no other,
Drinking wine by the bottle,
Making jokes about life?
Do you still feel the strife like we used to,
The overflowing fountain
Of unfulfilled dreams,
And do you still wish for more?

How long can one delude himself,
A temporary temple to
His very troubles?
From whence they came there's no sign,
Would he ever admit
Or wish to submit
To emotion as simple as sorrow?

Will he ever know the hurt
Built up from his actions?
His two-faced attractions
Lead him to nowhere again and again.
Would he care to see
Or would he just run on the breeze,
The easy retreat?

Remember the times, as they've gone,
The abusive ascension

To another dimension,
Seeming so high yet so buried
In a comforting bunker,
No one can enter, but
Will he ever escape the delusion?

R C Greenlow
[01.08.1995]

10 STALEMATE

She sits silently beside him,
Scowling into space
Nothing will erase
The cold, filling this warm room.
Doomsday naysayers swaying her,
He's praying her expression
Won't be the loaded weapon
In his harsh tones to come…

She's coming undone
Silently, violently, rapidly
Enslaved by the graverobbing
Daze that pervades every corner,
He feels like little Jack Horner
But outside the confines
Of childhood nursery rhymes.

"All the time in the world",
She hears her brain stutter,
He hears her softly mutter
Under her breath,
Yet cannot make out the words
He heard, lost but for her,
And he cries out,
If only to break the stalemate.

R C Greenlow
[03.06.2021]

11 BUTTERFLY MOMENTS

Will I make you too many promises,
Astonish you with love then admonish you?
I'm truly hoping that's not what I will do
With all focus and emphasis on the word, 'true'.

Like a butterfly my smile lasts not so long,
I often spend too long in my chrysalis,
I mean, listen to this ensemble of words
Do I listen to myself, or just what I heard?

As the Spring enters the apex of our thoughts,
The volume of love we've brought carries us
To heights above and through lows below,
The blows we absorb just make us stronger.

You and I, we're like butterflies,
With the choice, whether to live or die,
At any time willing to sacrifice our lives
For each other, if ever the need should arise.

Our future can only be an entourage
Of butterfly moments that always last,
Even after each and every love blast
We'll still fly together unaided and fast.

R. C. Greenlow
[04.03.2020]

12 THE SWARM

I imagine to be floating away,
Struggling through my minor wars,
Occasionally seeing more clearly
The obvious, insidious, unavoidable flaws.

Without any kind of prejudice I can see
Thinking deeply can be insane,
As I continue to ramble on
Into whatever may lie beyond the rain.

Shaking in despair, I shudder on,
Through uncertainty in raw form,
I guess I'm floating gently away
From the rat-race, the chasing swarm.

R C Greenlow
[11.06.2000]

13 MESSAGES FROM LIFE

When all is wrongs
Listen awhile to the songs,
You don't even need reasons
To be fleetingly floating away.

Stay awhile,
Relax, smile, and Karma
Times itself to exist in you,
And your soul knows it's true.

Take all you feel you've learned,
Yearned for change so long,
Burned at the stake for doing it wrong
For such a long, long time.

When all is calmer,
Karma returns once again,
As if it ever truly goes away
Or leaves your side, my friend.

R C Greenlow
[31.03.2008]

14 LEARNING CHANGE

Panicking, churning gut, turning around, yearning,
Reaching for the ceiling, the feeling unfolding.
Stifled by the racing, chasing and pacing,
It's all going to turn into nothing again.

Freaking out without restraint,
A broken up canvas on which to paint.
Learning that the yearning is mashing me up,
Feeling the unfolding paranoid crumbling,
Mumbling and muttering every complaint.

A silent sickness soaks my stomach
As I roll up my life into pieces of ashes
That fly on the breeze to the trees,
I freeze as disease and despair invade,
With icy cold fingers of death on my heart,
To remind me I play the integral part…

The future is up to me.

R C Greenlow
[15.06.2000]

15 DISCONNECTION DAZE

Ornately fashioned craft gin bottle atop the kitchen work surface,
Lying prone and heavy on your side with no trace of alcohol left within,
What say you of the way the bottle spun before the fun came to an abrupt end?
Remind me what fences may require mending prior to lending myself to the next drink...

Shiny new mottled blue RFID case hidden in the inside back pocket of my man bag,
Protective vessel for my eight indifferent perilous plastic debt enabling enslavement devices,
Oh what joyous reading of arbitrary figures on online banking screens have I to look forward to
With no accompanying steadying beverage to wash away the growing sense of entrapment...

Strong sleek lines, bold deep colours and a high-speed fibre optic broadband connection
Enshrines such an ultimately false sense of security, that coerces one to reach for yet further layers

Of information overload, big data exposures and a growing lack of composure about my privacy,
While I continue sharing selectively my creative endeavours to help me weather the storms…

Black metal and plastic digital flashing attractive smart adaptive contraption handheld in my palm,
Keeping me connected to the continuous emptiness and loneliness I find abundant in cyberspace,
What say you of real human connections, born of feelings and empathy from proper interaction?
Tell me how much time is wasted becoming further disconnected while the world passes me by…

R. C. Greenlow
[04.03.2019]

16 GRADUALLY COMING UP

It's been an hour now since we dropped
That sweet, sugary, magical stuff,
And the warm sunny day is breathing,
Gently the intensity is increasing.

Outside the world just looks miles away
Colours are growing as dimensions unfold,
A suggestion of the journey to come
In waves of living emotion.

The daylight streams in, we're safe inside,
Travelling without moving, for miles and miles.
Might we find ourselves at a higher point,
Or reviewing life in technicoloured smiles.

Shall we record the day and replay the ride
Or sit back, reflect and flashback for a while?
This day is blessed with adventures so wild,
From our vantage point here on the sofa…

R C Greenlow
[05.04.2007]

17 FLOATING DOWN TO LIFE

Now I'm floating down to my favorite places and old friends faces
I'm not joking around this is outstanding from where I'm standing
The sound of blood rushing around my system
Hits me in the heart, heart's pumping like a piston!

Listen... can't you hear the sound?

Astounded by the way things come together in this stormy weather
The very moment, and not before, when I finally store away my doubts and fears
And clear a path to the task ahead without further ado
I always somehow knew, even in darkened ceremonies old, I would get here!

It's my truth, can't you see?

They'll try to tell me I'm a lunatic
They try to grind down my resolve
They'll disbelieve me and deceive me
Yet I'll keep coming back again for more
They're trying to drag me down you see
Clearly, they fear the mere sight of me
So, I'll haunt them crazily and constantly
And consistently drive them to distraction!

The reactions I get from even a fraction of the old gits I used to call mates
Leads me further and further away from hate towards the light, my friends
Send me glad tidings and warm vibes every time we alight at each other's doors
And the best part of all is we stand tall together, not knowing quite what's in store!

Will you shake my hand, old friend?

Gimme' a hug and release all the bugbears you have about me, I can take it
Tell me your stories and share with me your secrets, I'll keep them
Hold me close to your heart right from the start and I promise never to

forget
The value, trust, honesty, respect, unity, love and peace that we share!

Do we all stand together in the end?

Some try to get involved
They're insufficiently evolved
They don't really get a look in
At the schemes we got cookin'
They're hopelessly lost outside
They'll try to run and hide
When we unite as one to become free
They'll shout at us as they flee!

Watch them point the finger at me!

R. C. Greenlow
[22.02.2020]

18 PAR FOR THE COURSE

Never easy is this life game you know,
And I know it's not meant to be simple
The trick is not to overthink everything,
Not to overcomplicate matters in hand.
It's all simply par for the course,
Of course it's still hard to absorb
But the hits can keep on coming
And I'll keep on rolling with them.

Hidden in depths of me nobody but I get,
I never forget the most important lessons
By learning from the mistakes I make
I can keep on keeping them all guessing.
I'm suggesting you can do the same,
Free your mind and heart from the shame
And refuse the guilt they choose to keep
On reminding you of every chance they get.

Nobody has the right to single you out
For criticism or judgement, so shout
Your rage from the rooftops if it helps
To get the anger out in a healthy way,
Just be careful not to cut those people
Who never made you bleed, you need to
Be mindful on how to vanquish with speed
The emotions that try to burn everyone.

Don't take me for some sort of preacher
But if you find wisdom then pay it forward
I'm no leader nor prophet nor teacher,
Just a man always trying to be ever better
At this game called life, the strife
And rhymes of a lifetime all kept inside
And only expressed when the time is right,
In the appropriate setting to shine light.

Be a beacon for others who struggle too
So that your experience might benefit them,
Hold your hands up high in light and truth
With a shining suit of armour to protect you.
Beware those out there who simply don't care,
For they are the toxins that poison us all
And prevent us from connecting together
Through even the worst of life's weather.

R. C. Greenlow
[29.02.2020]

19 POSSIBLE?

I'm exclusive, elusive, lucid.
Trying every day not to be abusive,
Sometimes wondering what the use is
And resisting the urge to blow fuses.

See me looking at you, all wide-eyed,
Entranced by your face when you smiled
Taking mental notes, later to be filed,
Quietly driving me fucking wild!

I like all I see, allow myself to feel,
Perhaps I might even try making it real?
If I spy the signs, reflected in your eyes,
I'll surprise you with a wished-for kiss.

I'm emotional, unconventional,
Unconvinced by most people's spiel,
Preferring simply keeping things real
And wonderfully, deeply mental.

Psychology, philosophy, they appeal to me,
Pressing down to and through depths
I previously wasn't even aware of,
Silently bubbling away, subconsciously.

That's how I can see clearly
You're definitely right for me,
Allowing hope to enthrall my soul
At the prospects and possibilities.

R. C. Greenlow
[13-12-2019]
Dedicated to Betsy.

20 WEIGHTLESS

As the balance in the palace of my thoughts
Morphs gradually north towards the light
I'm slightly shocked and awed, of course,
Yet totally calmed by the journey forward.

Balanced in this carefully nurtured palace
That's been engineered by my own volition,
My position shifts only to become ever calmer
Like a balmy sea, I certainly am afloat here,

Sincerely I mean, clearly the dream unfolds
And I'm all resolved and recovered, behold
The still blue of the ocean of my inner world,
As my dream swirls gently in the whirlpool,

Travelling northward, my basin empties slowly
Into the pipework and drains inside my brain
Journeying long round the maze, hazy dark
Passages that inevitably lead to the open sea.

Life is a ride so akin to this brain draining thing
As the nuts and bolts of other people threaten
To choke, I simply stoke up the fires of my soul
And take the whole lot to a place in my head

That feels and looks like bed, wooed to sleep
By sheer effort of will, yet still is my heart
And calm are my thoughts, I've bought myself time
To throw down these lines, to remind me I'm okay.

Today is a brand-new start, just like them all,
I will stand tall, I will deal with daily dross
Like a boss, fortified by the power of my mindset
Expecting the worst, prepared, but hoping for better

Doesn't matter about any kind of weather, I settle
For whatever life wants to throw my way, I sway
Occasionally before steadying myself with stealth
And willpower that fires up from my very core.

Bless those who guided me and continue to guide,
Bless the sky, the ground, the trees, the whole ride,
Blessings everywhere, blessings inside curses,
Bursting forward to reveal a better mindset for me,

Filling me with a natural euphoric headiness
That pleasantly accompanies me as I walk around,
Listening out for the sounds and signs all the time
Like a prophet waiting for signals from a god.

My spirit is being freed with no need for weed
Or chemical assistance, I'm creating my own existence.
Watch how I build up resistance to the pitfalls
And potholes that life insists on putting in my way.

Now is the time, the present moment, right here
There's no fear left inside me, I'm pretty much free,
No anxiety to hold me back and no depressive attack,
No way I can go backwards, I just keep on keeping on...

And this will be my song.

R. C. Greenlow
[21.02.2020]

21 BIG TIME ACTUALITY

Born, to be barely able to stay stable
For decades, then finally the haze fades
And I'm thrust into a maze of pillars,
Surrounded and shrouded by smoke and mirrors...

Awake so suddenly, standing upright
Somehow, despite the long dark night,
Legs hurting like hell, eyes looking wild,
Mind racing ahead like an excited child,
Right at the top of the craggiest hill
I stand, swaying slightly, with bitter pill.
Heart beats fast yet everything's still,
I'm fearing all may have been for nil...

This is my chaotic lifelong expedition,
Traversing through every single inhibition,
Conquering each and every pitfall,
Stopping, only to demolish a wall
Or two, truly embracing all terrain,
Learning to love walking in constant rain
Without succumbing to the crazy pain...
Wearing my heart on my sleeve no longer,
Even as thirst and hunger try to pull me under,
Nothing can hope to steal my thunder
Now I'm well and truly underway, the right way...

Delayed only by momentary temporary paralysis,
I'm almost embarrassed I've ravished this gift of life

With unnecessary strife, all balanced on edge of knife
But, in the final analysis, the savages outside
Never could touch the richness of the deep inner life
I've cultivated and cultured without respite,
In spite of all distractions, refracted through
The prism of who I thought I was,
To arrive much closer to who I can truly be.

Only now can I really see...
Do you see?

I see several ships in the harbour,
Whipping up a fair old lather over by the shore,
Of course, their skippers are now all divorced
From the ocean-bound orders & enforced sobriety
That formed their enormous disquiet abroad.
And just as the whole of me shudders at the thought
Of reports that I'm on it even worse than before,
My eyes widen, broadening in response to some hidden danger,
Stranger than fiction and even harder to narrate,
I swear down this old town keeps making me late...

As I accept I'm regrettably mad as a banshee,
They're all so utterly soft and squidgy underneath me
As I ruthlessly tread them right into the carpet of trust
I carefully developed, rusty from the heavy rain
And constant pain of simply maintaining Us...

R. C. Greenlow
26.09.2020 - 30.09.2020

22 FRESH FINERY

Togetherness abounds,
Surrounds us with arms encircled,
But is our love only local
And narrow like a meandering stream?
It seems I'm pondering
On what's next for us, wondering
If our metal will rust too soon
And reveal jagged red holes

If the finest things about me,
The things I find fine in you
Wear thin on appeal, even though
They're our best qualities,
What on earth are we to do?
What's left if we become bereft
Of fresh inspiration from each other
Despite all that we hold dear and true?

What if my worse qualities
Dampen your love too much,
Or I somehow suddenly tire
Of being inspired by your finery?
Not so sure there are answers
For these kinds of things, you know,
So, shall we continue leaps of faith
In square-footed trudging steps?

I hope I'm wrong to question
As I am, yet I know it's healthy
To have these questions in mind
So that we don't fall behind ourselves.
Goodness knows we need to be sure
Or as sure as we possibly can be
Because as true love's path twists
So the sands of time sift away too soon.

I'm content to be the best I can,
You the best version of you,
Keep plodding through the mires
To reach the lush, verdant grasses
It's what this journey together
Is all about, weathering storms
And always sowing seeds anew
To create our fresh blooms.

R. C. Greenlow
[02.05.2020]

23 FOR ONE LONG INEXPLICABLE WHILE…

Completely

Positive

Thinking

Steadily

Developing

Did you hear that noise?

Did you feel that creeping chill?

Do you feel nauseous and slightly ill?

Go to the medicine cupboard
And unscrew the lid from the little bottle,
Punch out a handful of little pills
To add to the dulling effect
And if your body tries to reject you
Just reach for that 'Jamaican sense',
And build a fence so tall,
A wall of towering strength?

Did you say that or just think it?
Did you pay for that before you drank it?

What happened to all those long, long nights
Of putting the world to rights?

I heard a noise, and felt the cloy chill,
Feeling nauseous and feverishly still,
Sweating a cold layer of fright.

R C Greenlow
[27.11.2006]

24 FORGOT MY GRATITUDE

I'm sorry guys, forgot my gratitude
For a moment there I got carried away
Forgive me, no excuse for being rude
It's my ignorance, it won't stay.

Forgive my faux pas and little incidents
When I get a little bit over-confident
Maybe it's a bipolar thing, I forget,
I don't get which malady is in play.

Flip the script, switch the vibe,
Realise, I never contrive to be snide
Maybe my kindness is a kind of weakness
Buried deep, the empath in me sleeps.

Thank to each and every single soul
That ever reached out unconditionally,
You all give me the strength that I need
To go on through life with positivity.

R. C. Greenlow
29.05.2021

25 HOLES IN THE OLD

I'M TRYING TO FREE YOUR MIND. BUT I CAN ONLY SHOW YOU THE DOOR. YOU'RE THE ONE THAT HAS TO WALK THROUGH IT.

It has become apparent
That I look at the spaces
Where you have been sitting
And lose myself in a trance
Like flower petals playing on the wind.

There's little fleeting visions
So solid for a second, silent
Until broken by interruption
And always so unique,
So I shift my eyes to avoid tears.

I never cry for sadness,
Never weep of suffering
And never fall slave to darkness,
Because the spaces you leave
Are really substance in the holes.

No matter how I feel,
The feeling is always there
To lift me from a fall,
Or guide me through
The problems I create but can't help.

In the everlasting changes
We see more often daily,
The spaces slowly start
To sing their virgin praise,
Rejoicing for the love all around.

R C Greenlow
[03.08.1995]

26 HOURS OF DARKNESS

Tell me I'm not wasting our time
Feels like I waste so much that's precious,
Realise you're again feeling threatened
And reeling from what I can say in rhyme,
As despite how much I wanna' be
It simply does not really suit me,
After all, you do know the score.

Lost in all but time, thoughts conspire
To trap me in old patterns of thinking,
I'd be more upbeat if we weren't sinking
And if my jaw wasn't held by this wire.
I'm tired of being the float
That holds up our love and carries us,
I'm throwing myself in front of the next bus,
Sure we somehow missed the boat.

The weight on our shoulders hurts,
Others are entering the fray of this
Blissed-out, worn-out, tired relationship
Where a lonely critic lurks,
Alone but for the hours of darkness,
When we're feeling cold in our harshness
And exchanging scowls, and dark flirts
Can court each of us while things are amiss.

R C Greenlow
[03.06.2021]

27 OBSERVED FLINCHES

The cower,
I'm sour,
Avoiding me for a spell
You don't have to yell.

I'm crimson,
You're oddly yellow,
A very pallid-looking fellow
Who prowls about
At night for their scraps.
Wow, must be crap
To be broken like that.

You flinch,
I'm sinch,
Easily sussed out
But never bossed about.

I'm golden,
You're platinum though,
Shining tower of strength
With a bench outside,
To hide from things.

I wonder that today brings…

R. C. Greenlow
[09.05.2020]

28 TESTY

My love, these things are sent to test us,
Wear them, bare them, try to rest up
And then work through the present moment,
Try not to worry about the past or future

I know you're used to fending for yourself
But realise it's no longer just you, it's us,
And I cannot help but be a part of the fuss
And bother, but it's no real bother to me love.

Realise baby I'm not here to be angry
Or cause you to be unhappy, I'm here for you,
To help if I can and to support if I can't
And to be a branch of this tree that you plant.
I'll always be here, I ain't going nowhere love
Don't you see how relief comes in having me
And I can be your partner if you'll let me be
Baby I only want what is best for you and me.

Testy mother fuckers and testing situations
Will always be a part of our everyday equation
But realise you're never alone in all this
I'm trying to help you when they take the piss
Let me be your anchor, your branch and root
I'll give you the support if you allow me baby
It's simple if you let it be, no bother at all
I'll be here forever for you, standing tall.

R. C. Greenlow
[16.11.2019]

29 THE NIGHT SHE LEFT

As the matrix rains letters, numbers and symbols down my screen

I begin to see the luminescent green streaks of code

Leaching out onto the walls and down onto the floor of my abode

Like the unfeeling tentacles of apocalyptic fear-inducing creatures,

Who's cold, unmoved, unswerving, ever-changing features

Seem to somehow penetrate my mind through the watery bulges of my eyes.

Though ultimately unsurprised at her departure at this time,

It seems to be beyond the reaches of my questioning mind

To be able to even know how I'm supposed to be feeling,

Or what in the name of all that is sacred I'm supposed to think,

Sinking as I am into a ham-fisted slam down to the ground

While nothing below me feels even remotely sound enough to land on.

A single feeble tea-light candle shines with its meagre flame

Next to me, as I type into this box on this screen, and I can't cry,

And I can't blame myself, yet I can't help but take the blame,

And strangely the overwhelming pondering thought remains:

How long will it be until the return of shame and fear take away

Every last bit of joy that I've fought all my life to feel for a day?

Green flashing hexadecimal, binary and ASCII code erode my senses,

As I wash down the bitter taste of defeat with the last gin of the week

Before slipping all but peacefully, no doubt fitfully into some sleep,

And await the nightmares that surely lurk there to jerkily scare me

Halfway to death and halfway to wishing for death, with every breath

I'm dreading the inky blackness that will refract my consciousness.

I don't blame her for believing stories told by those who
should know better,

Nor do I want her to see me hate this storm any more than
past nasty weather,

Whether I'm right or wrong I know their old song only too
damn well

And it's not for me to tell her who is gold and who is
merely gold-plated,

Any more than I would divulge to her the depths to which
I've hated them,

Where many men would poison back I hold off from any kind
of direct attack.

So, left bereft it seems, I cling to the idea of normal
dreams

Like the seams of some old witches twisted cloak, and the
idea is a bad joke.

I toke the choking ashes of trashy tobacco like it's going
out of fashion,

Whilst above and around me I'm surrounded by nothing more
astounding

Than the cold, bare floor I'm inevitably bound to
eventually land on

When I cease to be able to stand on this rocky arid ground
any more.

R. C. Greenlow
[25.11.2019]

30 THE ONESONG AGAIN

This Universal Consciousness
that some may call "God" is not a
separate, superior and condemning entity
as most religious institutions claim. It is in
fact the core essence of who we really are -
which is an all-knowing source that is of
Unconditional Love.

There's a certain song in the air...
Can you hear our fears evaporate there
Like vapour disperses into the atmosphere?
It's clear we're experiencing synchronicity...

My love has no boundaries or limitations;
It's raw powerful passionate perfectly healthy love,
The kind you always knew you'd somehow find
Just because you're kind to people all the time...

Karma sometimes needs a little helping hand see,
So I'm here to stir up the place, get things moving
Onwards, so we can all grow and rise, grooving
Together, ever building bridges and pathways...

R. C. Greenlow
[07.11.2019]

31 GYPSY GIRL

Living in loving ways with my gypsy girl beside me,
Totally spellbound, completely mesmerising, she
Makes everything feel completely fine, free
To roam, safely in our home, this is family.

Don't have to reach for her 'cos she's always there
My gypsy girl so warm, so kind and fine and fair,
She helps me lock in goodness and I'm accutely aware
Doing wrong by her I could never, would never dare.

She warms with her every intonation,
I make my time match my inclination
And armed with all the right information
I climb into the river of our love.

It's like a whirpool of naked emotion,
Her eyes inspire heartfelt commotion,
Demanding nothing less than devotion
Is sending us both rising above.

Ain't no chance of any more retribution,
Fucks too much with our inner constitution,
Those mofo's can flee the institution
But can never hope to touch us...

Never mind the fuss and bother,
We live and breathe dark down in Rother,
How could we hope to be any other
When they've funded our own bus?

Now is our time, as I rhyme in syndicate,
No time for tears, as I always indicate,
Ours is our own, l can only implicate
To you softly atop pillows of calm.

No harm can come to you any more love,
My Kingdom is all around, and above,
And below, and everywhere else, you see!
Your simply the one, the Queen of my sea.

Ours is a future to carve as we see fit,
Never mind all that past trauma shit,
Time is irrelevant anyway, my dear
You don't need convincing I'm sincere.

R C Greenlow
[19.06.2021]

32 ...THEN I LOOKED OUT OVER THE SEA

Chaos and confusion all around me
Interspersed with long verses of nothing,
Something dark deep down inside
Hiding from my realisations...
Backstabbing, heart-trampling people
Seem to be those towards whom I lean,
What does this mean for my wellbeing
And how can I avoid permanent hurt?

Why do I feel others think me needy
When all I want is to be loved unconditionally?
My thoughts so often end up down low
Despite all I do to try to be happy.
Life burns and breaks my will to try
And I so often feel simply cast aside,
So I hide behind these paranoid eyes
Trying not to show any kind of empathy.

I fail to be kind and I fail to be good
And I fail to be true too often by half,
The path to contentment winds uphill,
I'm only at the start of that path.
Euphoria always gets clouded by past trauma
Like paradise surrounded by hell,
And I'm hearing the tolling bell calling
A warning, but of what I cannot tell...

Then I looked out over the sea
And suddenly all was blissful within me,
The gentle waves lapped at my feet
And I immediately felt complete,
The smell and the sound and the sight
Were like reaching the end of a fight,
Despite all the pain still inside
I could finally smile at the ride.

When I looked out over the sea
Equanimity and peace enveloped me
The struggle suddenly became worth it,
Every single soul-shaking bit
The clouds above like all my worry
Dispersed as the day became sunny
And the warmth of that winters day
Came from within, not miles away.

R. C. Greenlow

[22.12.2019]

33 ALMOST TOO MUCH

Backwards, the hands of the clock tick
Forwards, onwards, ever ticking by
It sometimes seems the time is going
Far too fast, to complete every task
Of the day, yet also far too slowly?
Other things that could be getting done
Seeming to stay undone, the clock strikes
Soon, we'll soon be in need of sleep,
Again…

Sometimes the time becomes meaningless,
Unimportant, even unfathomable; yet
Its meaning never fades, the future's
Growing nearer, the absurdity of it all!
Somehow I've to find ways to cope,
And seem to be doing better, yet always
There's more things to be doing, always
Being mindful of those things…

R C Greenlow
[09.04.2007]

34 CHOOSE STRIFE

Passing time
Passes me on the right,
Past the vents
That exhume the pent up aggravation,
Passing me on my left
A man struggles to hurry
Stumbling clumsily as he tries,
I don't try to steady him at all.

Some buttons are pressed
Others are neglected completely,
When people choose only to address
The most immediate issues as they see them,
Watch out for the ones
Who are just waiting to talk
There's nothing new to report
In this semi-urban jungle.

Lonely old soul, tormented for fun,
Leaves fall from most trees, but not for some
Uncanny how some always know you're low
And time their tirades for when things don't flow

Is it even real, this love affair we share,
Wondering around the place worrying about despair,
You see it took me so many trees before I stopped shaking
Them and instead chose walking around and underneath.

Press another button, go on, I dare ya'
Watch just what it inspires in me,
Nothing good or desired that's for sure
And nothing to help the cold feel.

Stand with your back to the wind,
Remember the days when you were dead,
Instead of weeping and moaning
Just simply go lay down your head.

R. C. Greenlow
[17.05.2020]

35 WE CREATE OUR OWN KIND OF HEAVEN

It's a kind of illusion,
We're all lost in the same delusion,
Looking for an easy ride,
Expecting always to surf the tide
Of Life, and change;
We rearrange our arrangements,
We reorder our individual chaos,
Life, upon lives, all in turmoil,
We all come tumbling down…

Reverse your weary frown,
Don't allow anyone to drown
With you, avoid their sinking ship,
Whip you lives up into a frenzy
Of beautifully crafted unity,
All friends, standing together…
We must all unite;
Life can't be so many dark nights,
The lights fly around me now,
Attracted by my bright blue aura,
A plethora of wonderful dreams!

So, here I find myself, again,
Like there's no end to all this
And there's no answers to be found,
I can only hear the sound
Of silence, an sudden empty scream.

I don't remember my dreams
And what's more, I'm damn glad
That every single symbol,
Every obvious clue, any kind
Of possible pattern always exudes
Like sweat, across the bows of those
Who dare to ever forget
Just why we met,
Whatever reason that was!

Because I know;
Life goes on despite us all,
Light exists in every fall,

Mighty is the mind that
Keeps it all inside…

One cannot hide, nor don disguise,
Nor slide around, twitching,
Pretending to cope, yet
Constantly choking on life.

Lies and evil, perpetrated
By evil-doers, in suits of armour
Made from the finest fears,
And the firmest controls
Over all we hold dear,
Has excluded the human race
From learning the truth of Grace,.
And the heartbeat, rapid
And roaring in rapture,
At the final capture
Of each and every moment,
When we were wonderful
And life was heaven incarnate.

And yet, still, without fanfair,
I still manage to be too late…

Looking for something in the wind,
Feeling unquestionably unoppressed,
Spirits soaring high upon our naked auras
Beyond the bits and pieces of life,
Freed of the cradle, unhindered now,
We are wholly tuned into the Onesong,
How amazing, this Grace sent here,
Perfectly in time, this awakening!

Trusting in it all we move on up,
The air clear and fresh on our lungs,
Incredible to think that all this is true,
Consoling, knowing it's worth the work.

R C Greenlow
[06.08.2006]

36 JUST WALK AWAY

Easy to look outside you
At other's problems and pain,
Easier to reach out to them
Than to delve deep within your brain,
Easier to offer advice
Than take your own medicine,
Helping others to heal
Puts your shit in the pedal bin.

Thing is, things overflow
When we overlook our own
Impediments and issues
And it all quickly mounts up.
That's when crises occur,
As floods breach our levees
We find ourselves unsteady
And unable to really cope.

Beware the do-gooders
For often there's rot inside,
You'll get judgement and bile
If you dare question their motives.
Be selfless only to a point,
Don't end up neglecting your needs,
As those you help the most
May well be the first ones to leave.

Life's a delicate balancing act
But hell, we all know that,
The trick is to treat others
How we would have them treat us.
So when you do all you can
And they throw it back in your face,
Just turn your back and walk
And leave them to their disgrace.

R. C. Greenlow
[12.11.2018]

37 MOUNTAINS AND MOLEHILLS

When big storms blow in,
Buffeted by shocks and traumas,
I seem to make like a shark,
An automaton on a mission.
Yet the silly daily annoyances,
The hiccups that interrupt my flow,
Seem to trigger a disabling rage
That reduces me to tantrums.

What is it about the really big stuff
That inspires such coping abilities?
How do I traverse these mountains
With such innate calm and control?
And yet, what is it about the little things
That utterly disables my equanimity?
Why does every mole-hill I encounter
Trip me up, as if I'm as blind as the mole?

Give me crises, trauma and disaster
And I'll help you over the bridges I build,
I'm an island of calm, a refuge and shelter,
When surrounded by terror and strife.
Yet petty annoyances and minor niggles
Drive me to almost instant distraction,
And as all logic and reasoning evaporate
I'm left feeling like a two year-old child.

'Don't sweat the small stuff' I hear so oft,
As if that was the easiest thing in the world,
But the mole-hills that litter my daily life
Have become without doubt my Achilles heel.
So give me mountains any day of the week,
I climb and I conquer and I thrive,
But just leave the room when I lose my mind
Over the littlest things in the world.

R. C. Greenlow
Inspired by Nathaniel George
[11.11.2018]

38 FORWARD MARCH

Absolutely free
To be absolutely me,
It's all absolutely fine
Now I see it all so clearly.

I make no excuses,
Got my purpose and my uses,
But through past abuses
I've let my people down.

So this is me restating
There'll be no more hating,
No pointless time-wasting,
As there's so much to do.

I'll forgive myself, if you do,
Get on with what we're meant to,
Stand up for what's really true
And help others do it too.

So lean on my shoulder
And I will be your soldier,
As we gradually grow older
Together, ever onwards.

R. C. Greenlow
[05.11.2018]

39 LEARNING

Life is all about endings and beginnings,
The old has to die for new things to begin,
We're breathing through cycles of hope and fear
To try to clear a path to a future we can't see.

Clarity is in short supply, so we hide behind
The cold comfort of our outdated excuses,
But nothing good ever comes of our refusal
To accept that change is, ultimately, inevitable.

Incredible then, to imagine ever having not known
That what we reap in life is the harvest we've sown!
Alone, we design and manufacture our own destiny,
The rest of the story rests purely on our coping abilities.

I don't have answers to more than a mere fraction of things
That we all have to ponder and negotiate and decide,
If we are not to simply hide from the inevitable rising tide
Of life's meandering path towards the gaining of real insight.

One thing I truly do know for sure though is this fact;
That how we act is a reflection of our innermost thoughts,
So surely we ought to be always improving our thinking
In order to be rising up, instead of just slowly sinking.

R. C. Greenlow
[06.11.2018]

40 WALLED IN

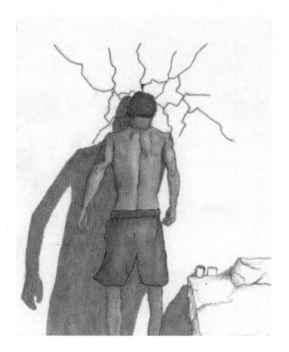

This is insane, isn't it?
Banging my head against walls
Built up over years and years..
Where once they protected me,
Now I am entombed.

Chipping away at the cracks,
Constantly hit by the flack,
I wipe dirty sweat from my brow
And wonder how I'll ever escape
At this slow rate.

My patience is running out..
I want to scream and shout
But only manage sneers and sighs,
And occasional cries
Of stinging self-pity.

My tools are all blunted
By the constant wear and tear

Of this relentlessly hard work..
I'd go berserk if not for
Lack of energy.

Tired of looking down,
But when I look up I get scared
By the height of those walls,
And the idea of scratching away
For all my days.

So, I slump back down
Once more to try to sleep,
Lapsing between confusion
And vivid nightmares,
In shades of grey.

R C Greenlow
[30.09.2018]

41 ALONE IN THE WORLD

It appears that somebody has tried to strangle me,
Just because I can't agree with their philosophy
Somebody else grates on me like new shoes on ankles
I'm losing all my sparkle but still keeping all my marbles.

Time has a funny way of waking you up to yourself,
Just when you think you've lost all your hope and health
Shaking your foundations, rocking you to pieces,
Then, when you can take no more, it suddenly ceases.

Openings in the brain welcome new ways of thinking
You can close them again if you feel yourself sinking,
But I'd rather play my cards one at a time tonight,
That way I can be sure that I'm doing it all right.

Life will avenge all attempts to hold back
From the throng, the joy, and the heart-attack
Better to seamlessly drift with the tide
Than surrender to the darkness held deep inside.

R C Greenlow

[04.05.2000]

42 NEVER POWERLESS

Here's something powerful for times when you feel powerless..
No matter what befalls us, regardless of nature or nurture,
There is always a choice, or there is no choice at all,
Either way, the same rules apply - the choice is to live or die:

To live is to absolutely dedicate yourself to choosing well
And be resolute in whatever course of action you choose to take,
Whilst owning any and all consequences and repercussions,
So that lessons can be learned and real improvement can be made.

To die is to accept something is beyond our current capabilities
And allow forgiveness for our inability, even if only by ourselves.
There is only really pride to be lost when we accept defeat,
And soon after comes a realisation that failure stimulates growth.

It is fear that prevents us from making the right choices,
Or from making a choice at all - fear of the unknown end result,
Fear of failure, fear of rejection by others, fear of change -
The fear of fear itself has us all tied up in terrified knots.

It's okay to be scared, but you cannot let fear rule your life.
You have to take the nervous energy of that fear and run with it
As fast as you can directly towards every goal you choose to set,

Or else you will get stuck in the mud and gradually sink below.

So stretch out those wings of yours, learn to fly with the wind.
There is a big old wide world out there and it's yours to enjoy.
Flock with others or fly alone, the choice is yours brave soul,
There's no time to waste and no reason to ever be grounded again.

R. C. Greenlow
[01.09.2008]

43 MANAGING CHANGES

It can all go to hell in a handcart
The moment you let go of the reigns of life
And rather like an undisciplined horse rider,
It's easy to hurt your stead and fall off.
It's wrong to try to run before you've learnt to crawl
And walking take momentous effort,
With your back up against the wall of your limits
You'll hit your head on rock more than once.

When you open up a path beyond the limits
Life usually expands faster than you'll believe
And you'll have to rush to fill the gaps
Before they're infiltrated by thieves in the night.
Taking hold of the reigns of your life
Will leave your hands sore with blisters,
And your head hurting, and your mind scrambled,
But atter you recover from the initial impact
You'll start to feel so much better than before.

Should you now have enough strength
To push the gaps and break through your walls
There's always someone to call on for help,
Somewhere surprisingly close by, you'll see!
If you get hung up on the pain, shove yourself
Down the road to righteousness, push hard,
As life won't give up it's beautiful secrets
Unless you give all your effort to the changes.

When others try to get in your way, don't allow
Them, nor curse them, nor push them away,
As they cannot truly understand your mission
Any more than you understand their complaints.
It can all change rapidly for the better,
And great things are just around the corner,
It's all about managing and working the changes
To ensure your life is going the right way.

R C Greenlow
[2018]

44 MOON-LINES

The parallel lines of gorgeous moonlight symmetry
Belie the daunting underbelly of the pain of me;
To be so completely in this reality, as portrayed by me,
Is burning at the edges of my very sanity.

No way is this moment just another one of those
So-called shortcuts that I did once propose,
Nor is this me once more meandering to a close,
No, this is the moment, right here, it's not verbose.

So, as I stare down the moon-lines, drawn on sea,
I'm thankful, for all that is only now open to me,
I say my small prayer and conclude, "Blessed Be",
For that, I know, is the way it was shown to me.

R C Greenlow
[15.07.2006]

45 CLIMB EVERY FENCE

Storms are over for now
How glad I am, couldn't stand
The constant torn, shattered dreams.
Seems easier on the other side,
And the gates are all open wide
For an interlude, so I need to use
This time as wisely as I can
Might not last, as I understand…

Pitch a fit, try not to rip
Apart the seems of the good start
You've made, you'll only be delayed
In the long process of rising,
Growing like it's adolescence again.
My pen quivers at the prospect
Of all the hard work to come.

You heal parts of yourself,
Only to find the next installment
Of pain and hardship rear its head.
Man it's crazy, the ride ahead
Speeds right through my head
And spurts out, spilling into consciousness.
It's not enough to relent or repent,
You have to be ready to climb every fence.

R C Greenlow
[09.05.2020]

ABOUT THE AUTHOR

Richard Greenlow has been writing poetry since his teenage years.

Following advice and help from his late Grandmother he decided to try to get some poems into print and has, three decades later, now released "The Strife And Rhymes Of A Lifetime", collection volumes one – three.

It is his hope that these books help those who, like him, suffer from complex mental and neurological issues, believe in themselves enough to try pushing their talents and abilities to the limit, and always strive to be the best version of themselves.

If there is an overall goal to Richard's writing it is to whisper into the wind and hope that others might hear, and in hearing, recognise something of themselves.

Printed in Great Britain
by Amazon